12 THINGS TO KNOW ABOUT
POLITICAL PARTIES

by Matthew McCabe

12 STORY LIBRARY

www.12StoryLibrary.com

12-Story Library is an imprint of Peterson Publishing Company and Press Room Editions.

Produced for 12-Story Library by Red Line Editorial

Photographs ©: Carolyn Kaster/AP Images, cover, 1; Henry S. Sadd/ Library of Congress, 4, 29; Scott Rothstein/Shutterstock Images, 5, 28; North Wind Picture Archives, 6; J. Aitken/ Library of Congress, 7; Shutterstock Images, 8, 26; iStock/Thinkstock, 9; Bettmann/Corbis, 10, 13; Shawn Kashou/Shutterstock Images, 11; Library of Congress, 12, 14, 15, 16, 18, 20; Charles Dharapak/AP Images, 17; Elise Amendola/AP Images, 19; Cliff Schiappa/ AP Images, 21; Brooks Kraft/Corbis, 22; David Duprey/AP Images, 23; Lisa F. Young/ Shutterstock Images, 24; Digital Vision/Thinkstock, 25; Susan Walsh/AP Images, 27

ISBN
978-1-63235-031-2 (hardcover)
978-1-63235-091-6 (paperback)
978-1-62143-072-8 (hosted ebook)

Library of Congress Control Number: 2014946809

Printed in the United States of America
Mankato, MN
October, 2014

Go beyond the book. Get free, up-to-date content on this topic at 12StoryLibrary.com.

TABLE OF CONTENTS

US FOUNDERS DID NOT WANT POLITICAL PARTIES

Political parties in the United States date back to the founding of the country in 1776. The people who led the American Revolution (1775–1783) were against the idea of political parties. A political party is an organized group. It tries to affect how a government is run. A party uses its political power to influence government policies.

Soon after the American colonists won the American Revolution, people began to form parties. For the first time, anyone had the power to influence politics. People organized into parties. They were able to express their political beliefs with more influence. Early leaders feared political parties would harm the country. George Washington and James Madison were against parties. They were afraid one party would gather too much power. These men believed that one party

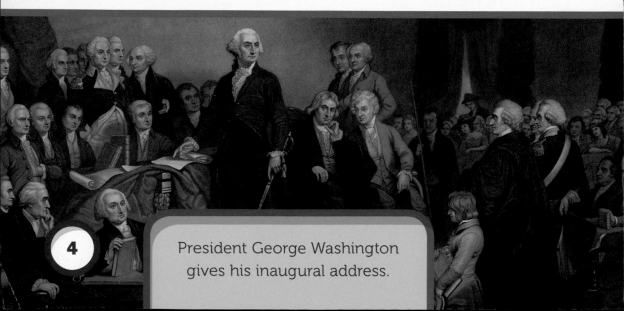

President George Washington gives his inaugural address.

It is difficult for one party to control all three branches of the federal government.

with all the power was no different from a monarchy. The nation had just defeated the rule of the British monarchy. People did not want to return to a similar government.

The US Constitution tried to limit the power of political parties. Power in the new government was divided among three branches. These were the legislative, judicial, and executive branches. One party could control one branch of the government. But it would be difficult for one party to control all the branches.

Early leaders hoped these political parties would be temporary. But today, those political groups still exist.

1
Number of presidents who were not members of a political party.

- George Washington was the only president who was not a member of a political party.
- The US founders viewed political parties as dangerous.
- The US Constitution tried to limit political parties.
- Political parties formed as groups fought for power.

THE ENGLISH CREATE POLITICAL PARTIES

The United States has had political parties since 1787. But political parties did not begin in the United States. They can be traced to England. English political parties started in the late 1600s. At the time, the English people disagreed about how much power the king should have. In order to gather power, people formed opposing groups.

King Charles II, who ended the English Parliament during his rule

Some in England wanted to kill King Charles II. This led Parliament to ban these people from serving in the government. But the king believed Parliament challenged his authority in taking this action. He ended the Parliament and ruled on his own until he died in 1685.

The English people took one of two sides. Some people believed the king was right. Others believed the Parliament was. The group that opposed the king was called the

"Whigs." The king's supporters were called "Tories."

The English people had two sides to choose from. On one side were supporters of the king's power. On the other side were supporters of more power for ordinary people. In the late 1790s, Americans also had two choices. They could vote for those who wanted a strong federal government. Or they could vote for those who supported stronger state and local government. Though less-influential parties have come and gone, these choices remain today.

109
Number of years between the founding of the first British political parties and the first American ones.

- The first political parties were formed in England, not the United States.
- The Whigs and the Tories were the first political parties in England.
- Political parties often represent differing sides of the same issue.

THINK ABOUT IT

Should one part of the American government have greater power? A strong federal government provides a single direction for national policy. Strong state governments offer greater control to the people of each state. What do you believe? Write a paragraph explaining your opinion.

An early English political cartoon showing the battle between the Tories (left) and the Whigs

EARLY PARTIES DEBATE THE ROLE OF GOVERNMENT

Early political parties argued two different views. On one side was the Federalist Party. Federalists wanted a strong central government. They believed the government should protect industry and help the country grow. Federalists were supported by US businessmen, banks, and merchants. John Adams, the second US president, was a Federalist.

On the other side was the Democratic-Republican Party. Democratic-Republicans wanted

THE FEDERALIST PAPERS

The views of the Federalist Party were first laid out in political essays. These essays were called the Federalist papers. US founders John Jay, Alexander Hamilton, and James Madison wrote the 85 papers. They promoted a strong central government. They also tried to encourage the states to adopt the new US Constitution.

John Adams supported a strong central government.

3

Number of electoral votes that decided the election of 1796 for John Adams over Thomas Jefferson.

- Political standoffs existed from the beginning of the United States.
- Federalists and Democratic-Republicans were the first US political parties.
- The two sides had differing views on the role of the new federal government.

Thomas Jefferson supported smaller federal government.

state governments to have more power. They believed the American Revolution was fought to free people from large and abusive government. This party was supported by planters and small farm owners. Thomas Jefferson, the third US president, was a Democratic-Republican.

These early political parties battled for control of the government. Each party had a different vision. Those different visions created early conflict among people in the United States. Opposing views and beliefs continue to define politics in the United States. Many of these early battles continue today.

4

POLITICAL STANDOFFS ARE NOTHING NEW

Elections in the United States today are very intense. Differences in opinion among voters create hostility between political parties. Today, political parties argue about issues such as immigration and terrorism. It may seem like these arguments are a new development. But political arguments are not a creation of the twenty-first century.

In the early days of American politics, elections were also intense. The problems the country faced back then were different. But they created the same hostility. The presidential election of 1796 was the first to feature heated political conversation.

Before 1796 George Washington had served as the first US president. His success and popularity during the American Revolution made him an easy choice. After he left office, a bitter battle took place over the presidency. Federalists, led by John Adams, wanted to continue Washington's work. Democratic-Republicans, led by Thomas Jefferson, thought the federal government was taking too much

The debates between presidential candidates Abraham Lincoln and Stephen Douglas were often intense.

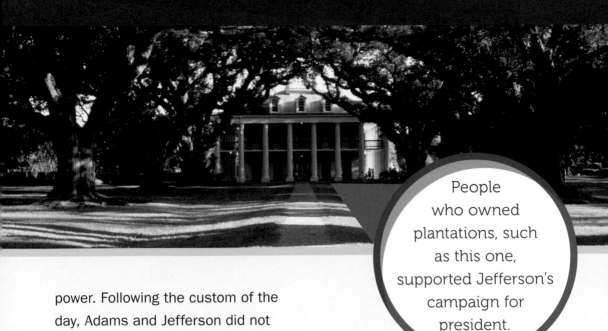

People who owned plantations, such as this one, supported Jefferson's campaign for president.

power. Following the custom of the day, Adams and Jefferson did not campaign themselves. However, their parties published newspapers to promote them. These newspapers fiercely attacked the opposing candidate. Adams narrowly won the presidency.

Federalists and Democratic-Republicans held different views for America's future. The views of each party were far apart and closely held. As political leaders fought for control, it became difficult to lead the nation. The opposing views pulled the country in different directions. The disagreement between the parties continued in the 1800 presidential election. This time, Thomas Jefferson, not Adams, won the presidency.

24

Number of years Democratic-Republicans controlled the US presidency, from 1801–1825.

- The US founders created the Federalist and Democratic-Republican political parties.
- The different parties intensely defended their beliefs.
- Early American politics was concerned with creating big government, or limiting the size of government.

POLITICAL PARTIES BECOME THE PEOPLE'S VOICE

Women's voting rights supporters march in New York City.

Very few people had a say in the first presidential election. Only white men who owned land were allowed to vote. Voting rights were limited this way until 1856. Early leaders believed people who did not own land did not have a stake in the country's future. But in reality, all Americans had an interest in the direction and health of the country.

6

Estimated percentage of the American population that was allowed to vote in the first presidential election.

- Until 1856 only white men who owned land were allowed to vote.
- The expansion of voting rights was a slow process.
- Women were not allowed to vote until 1920.

People other than white male landowners wanted the right to vote. Political parties gave people a way to fight for that right. Between the 1850s and 1920, the parties battled over whether minorities and women had the right to vote. These battles gradually led to these groups gaining that right. In 1856 all white men were allowed to vote. In 1868 former slaves were granted the right to vote. However, only black men could vote. Women of all ethnicities were not allowed to vote until 1920.

Black voters register to vote in 1966.

THE VOTING RIGHTS ACT

The Civil Rights Act of 1964 ended policies that denied rights to citizens. The policies denied rights based on race, skin color, religion, gender, or national origin. The Voting Rights Act of 1965 protected voting rights. It said individual states could not block any citizen from casting a vote in an election. Before this law, southern states were still trying to block blacks from voting.

TWO PARTIES HAVE DOMINATED US POLITICS

Two political parties have controlled US politics since the eighteenth century. But the names and goals of the specific parties have changed over time. Political parties come and go.

They become more or less influential. As the views and opinions of Americans changed, political parties changed, too.

For example, the Federalist Party lost influence after the 1800 election. Some people still believed

A political cartoon shows President Lincoln cutting down a tree representing slavery.

4

Number of presidents elected as representatives of the Whig Party, a precursor to the modern Republican Party.

- US politics has often been dominated by two parties.
- These parties have changed throughout history.
- The Democratic and Republican parties have dominated US politics for more than 140 years.

14

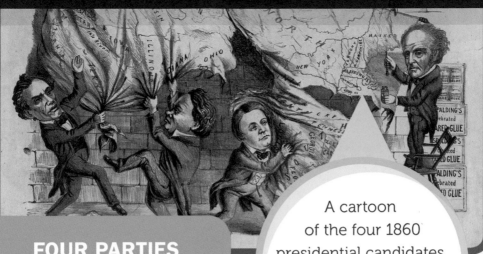

A cartoon of the four 1860 presidential candidates (left to right): Lincoln, Douglas, Breckinridge, and Bell

FOUR PARTIES OUT OF TWO

The 1860 presidential election was the only one to feature four major parties. Slavery and states' rights had split the parties. Democrats split into Northern and Southern Democrats. A new party called the Constitutional-Union Party had a representative. Abraham Lincoln represented Republicans and won the election.

in its views. But it lacked wide support among Americans. Twenty years after the 1800 election, the party had faded away.

In the nineteenth century, social issues often drew people to one party or another. Slavery and strong state governments were major issues. People in the American South and West were in favor of slavery and states' rights. People in the North wanted a stronger federal government and no slavery.

Today, US politics is still dominated by two political parties. Most voters identify as Democratic or Republican. However, many smaller parties also exist. They represent a wide variety of views and interests. But their influence is limited. Every US president elected since 1868 has been either a Democrat or a Republican.

THE CIVIL WAR CREATED THE MODERN PARTIES

No new major political party has been created since 1854. The Republican Party was the last major party formed in the United States.

Forming a major party is difficult. The success of a new party depends on strong feelings regarding social issues. The Republican Party succeeded early because of its stance on the issues of slavery and states' rights. These two issues were intensely debated in the United States in 1854. The nation was divided on these issues. Supporters of slavery in the North and South identified with the Democratic Party. They believed states should be able to choose whether or not they allowed slavery. Opponents of slavery joined together to form the Republican Party.

The schoolhouse where the Republican Party was first organized in Ripon, Wisconsin

Former House Speaker Nancy Pelosi hands off the gavel to new House Speaker John Boehner in 2011.

56
Percentage of Americans who identify as Republican or Democratic.

- Today's modern parties date back to the Civil War (1861–1865).
- The Republican Party was the last major party to form.
- Intense issues, such as slavery, are needed to help a major party thrive.

Today Democrats and Republicans continue to be the only two major parties in American politics. The issues that divide the sides are different. But the two parties cover most of the important social issues. This has prevented a third party from becoming a major factor in politics.

THIRD PARTIES ALSO PLAY A ROLE

Two parties usually dominate politics in the United States. But third-party candidates have impacted elections, too. They often represent people whose views are not covered by the two major parties.

The US Constitution does not limit politics to two parties. Sometimes people believe issues important to them are being ignored. They form a political party to get their voices heard. These parties often call attention to specific issues. For example, people who supported voting rights for women created the Equal Rights Party. Victoria Woodhull was the first presidential candidate for that party. She was also the first woman to run for president.

Sometimes the difference of opinion within a party creates a third party. There are two examples of this in American history. The first occurred in 1912. Theodore Roosevelt split from the Republican party to form the Progressive Party. The second occurred after World War II (1939–1945). Democrats from the

Victoria Woodhull addresses Congress on women's voting rights in 1871.

60

Percentage of the American population in 2013 that would like to see a major third party.

- Third parties have always existed, but have never been dominant.
- Third parties call attention to social issues ignored by the Democrat and Republican parties.
- The parties sometimes form after breaking away from a major party.

THINK ABOUT IT

Should third parties play a bigger role in politics? Some believe third parties are positive. Some see their impact as negative. Third parties can split voters who have similar beliefs. They can also draw attention away from bigger issues. What do you think? Use information from these pages to explain your answer.

South feared giving blacks more civil rights. Many members split from the party to join the States' Rights Party. This party was also called the Dixiecrat Party.

Third parties can represent a variety of viewpoints. The Libertarian Party promotes the rights of the individual and small government. The Green Party works to improve society's impact on the environment. Many others also exist. They all try to shift the government's focus to the issues important to them.

2012 Green Party presidential candidate Jill Stein hoped to focus the national debate on environmental issues.

THIRD PARTIES HAVE HELPED DECIDE ELECTIONS

Third-party representatives have been elected to state or local positions. But no third-party candidate has ever been elected president in the United States. However, these candidates have helped decide the outcome of presidential elections.

The Progressive Party split from the Republican party in 1912. Theodore Roosevelt was the presidential candidate for the Progressive Party. He got some votes from Republicans who believed in progressive causes. Other Republicans voted with their party. Republican votes were then split between the two parties. This helped Democrat Woodrow Wilson win the majority of all votes. He won the election.

TRIUMPHANT THEODORE

Theodore Roosevelt was the most successful third party candidate. He won 27 percent of the votes in America in 1912. No third-party candidate has earned such a large portion of the vote since.

Theodore Roosevelt campaigns in West Hoboken, New Jersey, in 1912.

More recently the Reform Party and Green Party have influenced presidential elections. In 1992, the Reform Party split Republican voters who had different beliefs. Some voted for the Reform Party candidate, Ross Perot. Most political experts believe this split helped Democrat Bill Clinton defeat Republican President George H. W. Bush.

In 2000, the Green Party split Democratic voters. Some voted for Green Party candidate Ralph Nader. Others voted for the Democratic candidate, Al Gore. As a result, many political experts believe, Republican

19
Percentage of the vote third-party presidential candidate Ross Perot received in 1992.

- No third-party candidate has ever won the presidency.
- However, third-party candidates have helped decide elections.
- Third-party candidates usually split voters of a majority party.

George W. Bush won the very close election. In each of these cases, third parties drew enough attention to issues to make a difference.

Ross Perot (left), George H. W. Bush (center), and Bill Clinton (right) greet each other before a debate on October 11, 1992.

PARTIES REPRESENT CONSERVATIVES AND LIBERALS

Supporters of the Affordable Care Act rally on the steps of the Supreme Court in 2012.

PROTECT MY HEALTHCARE.
PROTECT THE LAW
#protectthelaw

We ♥ ObamaCare
www.americansunitedforchange.org

61
Percentage of Americans who identify as conservative or liberal.

Politics today focuses on two general viewpoints: conservative and liberal. These terms are used to define the beliefs of voters. Whether a voter is conservative or liberal often decides his or her political party choice.

- Parties tend to represent liberal or conservative viewpoints.
- Liberal voters tend to believe government has a role in creating a society that is fair to all citizens.
- Conservative voters tend to believe creating a fair society is better handled by private citizens.

THE TEA PARTY

One political group that has made headlines in the 2010s is the Tea Party. The Tea Party is not a political party. It is a political movement. Most Tea Party supporters hold very conservative views. Tea Party supporters also tend to be white and older than 45. They are found across the country. More than half of Tea Party supporters also identify as Republican. Just five percent also identify as Democrats.

A conservative voter does not wish to see rapid changes to their way of life. Conservatives believe in individual freedom over government control. For example, conservatives prefer a small federal government. They do not want government making many of the decisions that impact their lives.

Tea Party protesters at a 2010 rally in Buffalo, New York

A liberal voter is one who believes the government plays a role in protecting individual freedom. They believe a strong federal government can help create equality for everyone living in a country. They place importance on government programs that help the public good.

Most conservative voters side with Republican candidates. Liberal voters tend to favor Democratic candidates. The terms have become closely linked to political parties. However, that does not mean conservatives have to support Republicans. Neither do liberals have to support Democrats.

23

THE ELECTORAL COLLEGE WAS A COMPROMISE

The founders of the United States could not decide how to elect a president. Should Congress vote for the president? Or should the American people vote directly? Instead of choosing one method over the other, they compromised. They came up with a system called the Electoral College.

The Electoral College is not a place. It is a process. It gives states a number of electors based on their population size. The electors vote as representatives of the people who live in the state. That number also determines how many people represent the state in Congress. Citizens in each state vote for a candidate. The candidate who wins the most votes in a state gets its electoral votes. To become president, a candidate must win at least 270 electoral votes nationwide.

Some people believe the Electoral College does not fairly represent voters. Electoral votes do not represent the popular choice of voters. The votes of all citizens together are

A state's electoral votes are awarded to the candidate who receives the most of its citizen's votes.

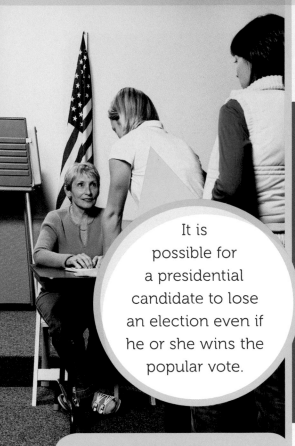

It is possible for a presidential candidate to lose an election even if he or she wins the popular vote.

THINK ABOUT IT

Does the country need the Electoral College? Critics believe it prevents people from voting. Those who think their voice is not heard often do not vote. Others believe it creates political unity in the country. Take a side. Write a paragraph explaining your opinion. Use these pages to support your answer.

538

Total number of electoral votes in the Electoral College.

- Americans do not directly elect their president.
- Each state has electors who vote as representatives of the state's citizens.
- The Electoral College has benefits and drawbacks.

called the popular vote. It is possible for a candidate to win the popular vote, but lose an election.

But supporters of the Electoral College believe it improves the voting process. The electoral system supports the two-party system. It forces candidates to develop popularity across the nation. Without the Electoral College, candidates could win with support from just a few regions.

POLITICAL COOPERATION IS POSSIBLE

Now, as in the past, differences divide political parties. These differences can make it hard for both sides to work together. At times, little progress is made in government. Today both political parties agree on the issues that impact America. Issues such as immigration, the economy, and welfare are important to both sides. But the parties have different ideas on how to solve the issues.

To make progress in solving any issue, it is often necessary for the parties to compromise. In a compromise, members of the political parties work together. They give up some of what they want to find a solution that will work for everyone. One example of compromise occurred in December 2013. President Obama signed a new budget into law. The details of the budget were a compromise.

It is possible for the political parties to cooperate.

Democrats and Republicans worked together to fund federal government programs.

Sometimes politicians find it difficult to compromise. They feel they are going against their beliefs and values. They feel doing so makes the people who voted for them unhappy, too. In October 2013, the federal government shut down for 16 days. Democrats and Republicans could not agree on a budget for the federal government. Federal government programs were shut down while they

A sign announces the National Parks closing due to the October 2013 government shutdown.

National Park Service
Department of the Interior

Because of the
Federal Government SHUTDOWN,
**All National Parks
Are CLOSED**.

tried to solve their disagreement. The shutdown ended when Democrats and Republicans agreed on a plan. They would negotiate the budget over the coming two months. The budget compromise in December 2013 was a result of this plan.

Though the sides disagree on how to solve issues, goals can still be achieved. For example, leaders from both sides agreed to change the Veterans Affairs healthcare system. Both sides made compromises to solve an issue that each viewed as crucial to the country.

23
Number of public laws enacted by the 113th Congress, the fewest in modern history.

- Both sides disagree on how to solve issues, slowing down progress.
- Finding a middle ground is tough.
- Bipartisan solutions require a compromise on the issues.

FACT SHEET

- Women's Suffrage is the popular name for the movement to grant women the right to vote. The 19th Amendment to the Constitution officially gave women the right to vote. The amendment was passed on August 26, 1920. But the movement to grant women voting rights began as early as 1848. The movement began to gain steam after the Civil War.

- In the mid-1900s, there were still places in the country where Americans were denied basic rights. These rights were often denied because of race or skin color. Blacks faced many struggles to gain voting rights. Before the Civil War, many free, land-owning blacks were denied a vote based on their skin color. Black men were allowed to vote before women were. Black women were the last to gain voting rights.

- There is no official Independent Party in the United States. Sometimes, candidates for offices at local, state, and federal levels run as Independent Party members. Independent candidates will often vote with both Democrats and Republicans, depending on their view on a particular issue. Independent candidates are seen as being moderate, rather than strictly conservative or liberal.

- Even though it is not an official party, there are roughly 24 million registered voters in the United States who identify as Independent. These voters do not identify as Democrats or Republicans. The largest third party in the United States, by number of registered voters, is the Constitution Party. There are 367,000 registered voters in the Constitution Party.

GLOSSARY

compromise
A settling of a disagreement by each party giving up something it wants.

constitution
The basic beliefs and laws of a nation, state, or social group that establish the powers and duties of the government.

dominated
Controlled.

electoral votes
Votes made by members of the Electoral College.

hostility
Great unfriendliness or opposition.

moderate
Not extremely conservative or liberal.

monarchy
A form of government rule where one person has power, usually a king or queen.

Parliament
The highest legislative body in Great Britain.

policies
Courses of action the government takes.

political
Guiding or influencing government policy.

FOR MORE INFORMATION

Books

Behrens, Janice. *Let's Vote on It!* New York: Children Press, 2010. Print.

Grodin, Elissa. *Everyone Counts: A Citizens' Number Book*. Chelsea, MI: Sleeping Bear Press, 2006. Print.

Krull, Kathleen. *Lives of the Presidents: Fame, Shame, and What the Neighbors Thought*. Boston: Harcourt Children's Books, 2011. Print.

Websites

"The Origins and Functions of Political Parties," Grolier Online
www.scholastic.com/teachers/article/political-parties

"Political Parties," Congress for Kids
www.congressforkids.net/games/Elections_politicalparties/2_
politicalparties.htm

"Political Party Time!" US Kids
www.uskidsmags.com/blog/2012/11/06/political-party-time

INDEX

About the Author

Matthew McCabe is a freelance writer with years of experience. He has written several magazine articles, contributes to business blogs, and creates marketing content for numerous businesses. He lives in Plymouth, Minnesota.

READ MORE FROM 12-STORY LIBRARY

Every 12-Story Library book is available in many formats, including Amazon Kindle and Apple iBooks. For more information, visit your device's store or 12StoryLibrary.com.